W9-BYF-944

This book is conveniently bound with open flat binding. The first and last page are glued to the cover to make it even more durable.

Another 500 Heartwarming Expressions

For Crafting and Scrapbooking

by Sandy Redburn
Artwork by Suzanne Carillo

Lettering by Suzanne Carillo, Shelly Ehbrecht & Diana Haines

Crafty Secrets Publications
15430 78A Ave.
Surrey, B.C. Canada
V3S 8R4

ISBN 0-9686648-2-2   Printed in Canada

Table of Contents - Book 3

Themes for Border & Expression Pages

For more inspiring ideas please visit our web site at **www.craftysecrets.com**
and sign up for Sandy Redburn's newsletter called,
'Creative Ideas Using Heartwarming Expressions.'

Introduction

This newly revised book is now even more jam-packed, with over 550 hand lettered expressions and hundreds of whimsical designs in a variety of favorite themes. By eliminating some of the enlarged alphabet pages and spreading the best of the 'Photo Quip' expressions throughout the book, I was able to add eight brand new pages. Check out pages 12, 13, 28, 71, 80, 81, 85 and 86! Several pages have also been up-dated with some new or re-done expressions and designs. For the first time, this book also has color samples of nine inspiring projects on the back cover!

Our sales show the biggest buyers of the Heartwarming Expressions Books are people using them for scrapbooking, followed by a wide range of various crafting mediums. Therefore, the newly revised Books 1, 2 and 3 will still include the words; Heartwarming Expressions for Crafting and Scrapbooking, but the words 'Painting and Stitching' are being dropped from the titles.

As many of us look for ways to add more simple pleasures to our often complex and stressful lives, we have begun to focus more on what's truly important - our family, friends, spirituality, health and homes. Adding heartwarming and humorous expressions to our gifts, greetings, scrapbooks, seasonal and home décor projects is an easy and fun way to create more warm fuzzies and smiles. When you stop to think, what better way is there to grace someone's life, than with a hug from your heart?

I hope this third collection of expressions will leave your imagination and creative spirit brimming with inspirational ideas. Have fun spreading smiles! *Sandy*

The People Behind These Pages

I'm **Sandy Redburn** and my dedication to inspiring others' creativity includes writing, publishing and teaching since 1993. As the author and publisher of the Heartwarming Expressions Books, I've become addicted to creating new expressions, or finding wonderful quotes and dreaming up innovative ways and places they can be used to add more heart appeal to life. Scrapbooking has become my favorite hobby.

Shelly Ehbrecht displays her talent in hand lettering by adorning these pages with her beautiful printing. Shelly has contributed greatly to this book from its birth, helping to make it all possible. An RN, she has also received her CPD, (Certified Professional Demonstrators Diploma) and also enjoys teaching folk art painting classes.

Suzanne Carillo, owner of Bisous Graphics is the main contributor for the artistic lettering and most of the illustrations, including the cover artwork in this revised edition, as well as the other Heartwarming Expressions Books and Stickers. Her artistic talents are show-cased in every style, from adorable to stylish heritage themes. The humor and whimsy she captures in her artwork is sure to make you smile.

Other Contributors

Diane Pruss, owner of Splash Graphics has done the typesetting and created the marketing materials for all of the Heartwarming Expressions Books and Stickers.

Cindy van Koll, a talented scrap-a-holic, helped create and photograph some of the samples for this book. Cindy also came up with the adorable baby announcement idea featured on the back cover.

Diana Haines, a calligraphy artist and teacher, has hand lettered several wonderful expressions throughout this book.

How To Make This Book Work

You Get To Decide

The best thing about the Heartwarming Expressions Books is that they can be used in so many versatile ways depending on ones interests, skill level, budget and imagination. You can simply use this book for ideas, when you can't think of what to say on a scrapbook page or card and then hand letter, or type expressions out in stylish computer fonts, or use alphabet stickers or die cut letters to spell out words. Other people prefer to trace or photocopy the expressions and designs to decorate an endless variety of surfaces. The great part is you can choose your favorite colors and the supplies to suit your style and needs.

Thanks to technology, we now have so many innovative supplies, techniques and possible surfaces available to decorate, it can make your head swim. This book is geared towards scrapbooking and paper crafts, as these two categories now represent the biggest buyers of the book. Although, if you check out my list on the inside front cover for '99 Places To Put an Expression', you will see a multitude of places you can put expressions to add heart appealing personality to all kinds of items. If you become inspired by the ideas in this book, look for more in-depth books, visit web sites, take classes and discover the full creative potential that different crafts can offer.

Copying Our Designs

With the purchase of this book, you can freehand, trace, scan or photocopy the expressions and designs for your own personal use. **You don't have cut the pages of your book up!** Tracing can be done on a light box or you can use a bright window. This book is bound using open flat binding, but if you are tracing a large or intricate design it will be easier if you make a copy of the page. An easy way to trace directly from this book, is to simply lay a sheet of vellum over any expression or design and trace over the lines. For anyone not familiar with vellum, it is the translucent paper I used for the candle wraps shown on the back cover.

You can also have the expressions and designs you want to use enlarged or reduced on a photocopier for pennies and use them like clip art. To prevent any show through from the other side, place a black piece of paper on the back of the page being copied. From your copy, cut out what you need and lay it out on plain white paper and glue with adhesive. I love Zig 2 Way Glue Pens because they allow you to remove and reposition everything. I used them to glue every expression on when putting this book together! Photocopy your layout page onto your final good paper or cardstock. You can make copies on colored or plain paper and color them.

One of my favorite ways to cheat, is to make color copies of my finished scrapbook pages in reduced sizes to create magnets and cards, or have them copied onto vellum to make candle wraps. You can see two candle wrap ideas on the back cover, with directions on pages 16 and 66.

Putting Expressions on Various Surfaces

Depending on your project, you may want to transfer expressions from this book onto fabric, garden stones, wood and more. You can have the expressions and designs you want to use enlarged, or reduced in size. Place a sheet of graphite or transfer paper between the image and your prepared surface and trace the outline with a stylus or empty pen tip. Saral® manufactures a wax free transfer paper that works on ceramic, fabric, glass, metal, tile, wood, etc. Wax free paper will not clog the tips of your markers and pens. Heat activated transfer pencils also work well on fabric.

Easy Lettering
Tips & Tricks

You may see some expressions or have words you want to use, that you want to hand letter yourself. Many people don't like their own handwriting, but it is uniquely you and it's worth becoming more comfortable with. If you follow some of the simple tips given here, you will see your lettering skills improve with a look that is more consistent, easier to read and visually appealing. Some helpful tools for hand lettering include a soft lead pencil, clear ruler, good art eraser, and whatever pens or markers you want to use to ink any lettering once you're happy with it.

First pencil some lines out and practice lettering some words to get the spacing and size right. Words don't have to be even or straight, but try for consistency between the letters and words. When lettering on a scrapbook page or card, you may want to do it on a separate piece of paper or cardstock.

It's Easy! with Practice & Patience!

This way you can easily toss mistakes. Once it's inked, it can be trimmed and matted for a nice touch. When inking lettering, hold the pen upright and pull it towards you rather than pushing it away for better pen control. Pens now come in a multitude of tip styles, sizes, colors and effects. I love the new glitter pens! Water based pens work well for many paper crafts, but permanent Pigma ink pens won't fade and can be used on a variety of surfaces.

You can add emotion and personality to words by the lettering style you choose and the embellishments you add. As you can see in the samples below, although they are only words, each one conveys a feeling associated with the word. This book is filled with all kinds of lettering styles to inspire you. All you have to do is get creative!

Creative Possibilities

Expressions on Glass & Ceramics

You can paint expressions on an assortment of dishware, tiles, vases and décor. You can use traditional ceramic techniques and glazes, or cheat and use the new glass and ceramic paints that can be air dried or baked in an oven to produce a durable finish. The painted mug on the back cover would make a fabulous birthday gift for a golfer. The pattern and directions are on page 48.

Expressions On Wood

If you like working with wood, you have a whole range of creative possibilities for painting, carving, wood burning, decoupage and more. Visit any craft store to get inspired, or look around your home for items you can transform. There are also all kinds of innovative supplies that can help make you look like a true artist! For example, if you want to create garden signs and you don't have a steady hand for painting expressions with a paintbrush, don't worry. There are some great tools like all-weather paint pens and markers that make lettering so much easi-er. I revived an old picnic table, by enlarging the Expression 'Have a Bloomin' Good Day' (page 43) by 200% and painting it around the table rim with a green Marvy Paint Marker. I finished off the project by stamping flowers and dragonflies with foam stamps dipped in all weather Patio Paints on the tabletop. Just imagine all the things you can recycle!

Expressions On Fabric

When painting fabric, pre-wash it and don't use any fabric softener. You can use fabric transfer paper, or a heat activated transfer pencil to put the images on. Use fabric paints or regular acrylics mixed with a textile medium. Look for quality brushes recommended for textile painting or fabric markers. The mini tips on fabric paint bottles also work great to do lettering. You (or your copy center) can also scan and print images from this book along with photographs and print them on fabric iron-on sheets. These 'printer friendly' fabric sheets can be ironed on clothing, pillows, memory quilts and more. * Remember any lettering must be mirrored or it will print backwards.

Expressions For Paper Crafts & Scrapbooking

You can use these expressions to create your own special occasion and seasonal decorations, birthday cards, scrapbooks, framed layouts, greetings, gift tags, invitations, stationary, wrapping paper and more. There are so many cool things you can use to jazz up your work. Try using colored pens, pencils, buttons, charms, decorative punches and scissors, ribbon, stencils, stamps, wire, nostalgic keepsakes and... our NEW Heartwarming Expressions Stickers! Our new stickers are printed on acid free clear sheets and include some favorite expressions from the four Heartwarming Expressions Books, along with brand new artwork by Suzanne Carillo that ties in great with the books. At this time we have eight different sheets and we will be introducing eight more in summer 2002.

Coloring is Great Stress Therapy

Colored pencils provide an easy, very portable and inexpensive way to add personality and an artistic flair to journals, handmade cards, scrapbook pages and other paper crafts. The most common colored pencils, are the pencil crayons kids use in school and they are usually wax based. There are also watercolor and oil based colored pencils. My oil pencils, made by Walnut Hollow, work great on wood.

Watercolor Pencils have become my favorite colored pencils to use on paper. I now happily own a set of General Pencil, Prismacolor and Staedtler watercolor pencils. Your choice of paper is really a personal preference, but keep in mind, regular paperweight can buckle easily if it gets wet. Be stingy with water when blending colors and test on scrap paper first. Add color in layers, starting with the lightest and shading with darker tones. Try the different coloring techniques below to see which you prefer.

- Stroke a wet brush or blender pen across the tip of the pencil, or in a patch of color scribbled on scrap paper and then paint your image.

- Color your design with dry pencils and then blend the colors afterwards using a small paintbrush, a damp Q-tip, sponge applicator, or a blender pen.

- Color directly on paper, shading and blending colors the same way you would use regular pencil crayons and not even use any water.

Decorator Chalks are my other favorite medium for coloring with. They blend beautifully and if you don't like a color or you've gone outside the lines, simply use an art eraser and start over. You can also use colored pencils or felts to create vivid colors and then use chalks to add softer colors. Decorator Chalks can be found at most craft and scrapbook stores. They come in palettes with squares of colors and they usually include a pointy and round sponge applicator to color and blend with. I buy extra eye shadow applicators in bulk at the dollar store so I have one for each color.

Blender Pens are so versatile and easy to color with. They look like felt pens and normally contain a refillable liquid (I'm told a mix of glycerin, water and alcohol). Some brands include Dove, EK Success, Marvy and Tombow. The pointy tip styles are perfect for coloring tiny details. To change colors, simply stroke the pen tip across scrap paper until the fluid runs clear and pick up a new color. They can be used in many ways and with different products as you will see in the various applications I've listed below.

- I love using a Blender Pen to color with chalk. Dip the pen tip into one corner of a chalk palette and 'paint' with the pen tip. Not only can you paint with chalk, the blender pen will seal the chalk! Always use the same corner in each square of chalk.

- Rub a blender pen across water based felt tip pens to pick up the color, or scribble a patch of color with a felt pen on an old plastic lid and dip a blender pen in it.

- Dab a blender pen on a colored inkpad and color away.

Life is heavenly when you have ANGELS for FRIENDS

Guardian Angels from up above Please watch over those we love

Angels bring comfort from up above, on wings of faith and whispers of love

Sweet enough to be an angel

A FAIRY enchanting time

Angels are messengers from above, sent to spread God's light and love

DON'T WAIT to act like an ANGEL until you get to heaven

A wing and a prayer can take you anywhere

A fairy nice person & an old troll live here

Be an angel, God loves a helping hand

9

Our Little Angels

Miss Angelic

Master Saintly

Sweet Baby Cherub

Angel Magnet Directions

(pictured on back cover)

Copy page on white cardstock. Use chalks or watercolor pencils to color. See pg 7 for coloring tips.

Trace wings on pearl vellum using a gold or silver pen. Attach wings. Cut photos of children's faces out slightly larger than the pattern and glue to each angel. Cut out angels and add magnetic tape to backs.

For protection, laminate or cover with clear sticky contact paper. Note: These magnets were made by simply making a reduced color copy of the finished scrapbook page

When I think of Angels I think of you.

Angels help radiate his love from above.

Fairy Duties
☆ Watch Over Children
☆ Sprinkle Sleepy Dust
☆ Collect Lost Teeth
☆ Listen to Hopes & Dreams

My Guardian Angel watches over me and keeps me safe as safe can be

When the first baby laughed, for the first time, his laugh broke into a million pieces, and they all went skipping about. That was the beginning of fairies.

Freckles are Angel Kisses

Good Night Sweet Prince (Princess) and flights of angels sing thee to thy rest.

Wish I May, Wish I Might See a Wee Pixie Tonight

Secret Garden Fairies Gather Here

11

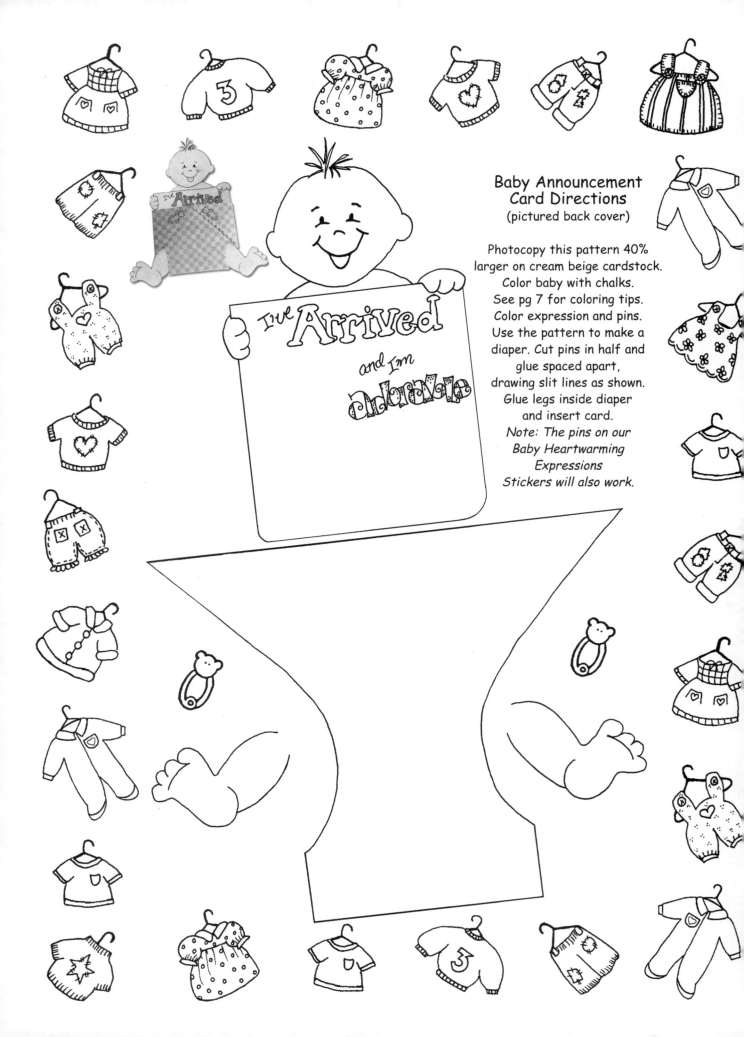

Baby Announcement
Card Directions
(pictured back cover)

Photocopy this pattern 40%
larger on cream beige cardstock.
Color baby with chalks.
See pg 7 for coloring tips.
Color expression and pins.
Use the pattern to make a
diaper. Cut pins in half and
glue spaced apart,
drawing slit lines as shown.
Glue legs inside diaper
and insert card.
*Note: The pins on our
Baby Heartwarming
Expressions
Stickers will also work.*

I've Arrived
and I'm
Adorable

Babies Smile When Kissed by an Angel

BABY LOVE

You created my inmost being.
You knit me together
In my mother's womb.
- Psalm 139:13

I'm the BABY Ya gotta Love Me!

God's Smallest New STAR

Babies are bits of stardust blown from the hand of God
- Larry Barretto

Little BOY BLUE we LOVE YOU!

Babies are such a nice way to start people.
- Herold

PARTY
When: 2am
Where: my crib

Its Hard to Be Humble when You're the Grandparents

NAME THAT FOOD

SMART Baby TRICKS

FROM a Little Babe So VERY SMall HOW & when did you GROW so TALL?

I'M A BIG Tipper

BABY
DINNER'S ON ME!

13

There Is A Special Blessing In My Life: You

Blessings

Count Your Blessings Every Day & See Them Grow In Every Way

Lord Let Your Love and Grace Shine Upon and Bless this Place

Were there no God, we would all be in this glorious world with grateful hearts and no one to thank

- *Christina Rossetti*

Choose Joy!

May all the world be richly blessed With lasting peace and happiness

God loves us Pass it along

Fond Memories of Friends, Family & Fun times

For today and its blessings, I owe the world an attitude of gratitude

May the road rise up to meet you May the wind be at your back.

- *Irish Blessing*

Each day is a gift to unfold Life!

Cherish each one, because the present has no mold

15

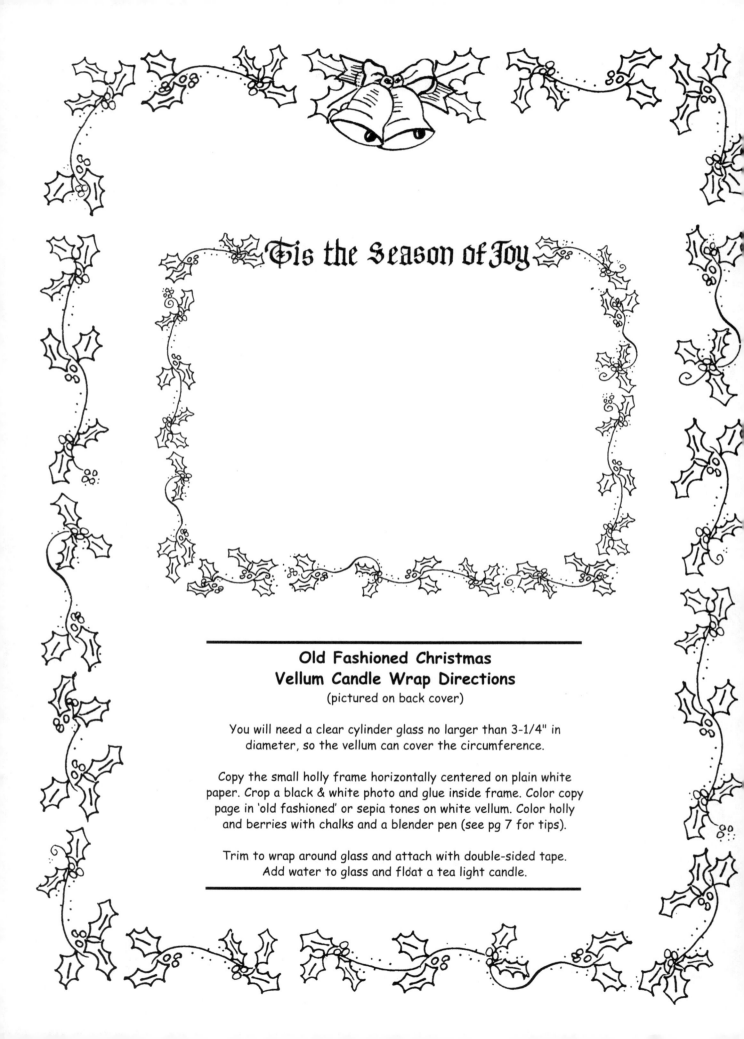

Tis the Season of Joy

Old Fashioned Christmas
Vellum Candle Wrap Directions
(pictured on back cover)

You will need a clear cylinder glass no larger than 3-1/4" in diameter, so the vellum can cover the circumference.

Copy the small holly frame horizontally centered on plain white paper. Crop a black & white photo and glue inside frame. Color copy page in 'old fashioned' or sepia tones on white vellum. Color holly and berries with chalks and a blender pen (see pg 7 for tips).

Trim to wrap around glass and attach with double-sided tape. Add water to glass and float a tea light candle.

Winter Wonderland

 CHRISTMAS

Peace on Earth
& Goodwill to All

Christmas Blessings
wrapped in warm wishes
tied with joy &
sent with love

Berry
Kissmas

Wise men still adore Him

CHRISTMAS IS
SNOW MUCH
F*U*N

Tis
the Season
of Joy

Joy

EveryONE
is a KID at
Christmas

SANTA EXPRESS

Season's Tweetings

Wishing you a Christmas brimming
with love, laughter and joyful memories

Be good for goodness sake

OFFICIAL Grinch

The Perfect Man
He's quiet and sweet
and if he gives you any grief
you can bite his head off

Santa's Workshop
Elves' Entrance

17

There's snowman I'd rather be with. CHRISTMAS.

There's Snowplace Like Home For The Holidays.

Cold nose... warm heart.

Yo*Snow

Shaped from warm hands and young ♡s

There is snow-girl like my girl Frosty

Be warm Inside & Out

Chill out! I'm a really cool guy just a little bit flakey

WANTED Summer house to rent Freezer space preferred

The Christmas present most often returned LOVE

To my Family:

May the spirit of Christmas fill you with love and peace, spreading goodwill that will never cease.

Yule always be the best part of Christmas xox

Deck the malls... with all my money.

Who Needs Santa? - I Have VISA

Like a Snowflake You're one of A Kind

Don't get yer knickers in a knot!

We had an Udderly Moovelous Time

Good Moo's from the Herd
We've added one udder.

HOME ON THE RANGE

Happiness is...
Being a True Cowgirl

Please tell my Mom:
Cowboys don't take baths,
We just dust off

Welcome to the Ranch

☆ Sherrif on Duty ☆

Howdy

You're the apple of my eye,
You're the cream of the crop,
You're the ice cream on my pie
and the cherry on top!

JUST HORSIN' AROUND

Bless The Birds & The Bees

So many frogs... So few princes

Lady Bug...Lady Bug Where have all the men gone?

Welcome to our PAD

DON'T BUG ME!

Toadly Hoppy

Frogs get to Eat whoever bugs them

Bless Ewe

To BEE or not to BEE......

Ewe wooly warm my ♥

Have you HERD the MOOS?

There will never be an udder quite like you ♥

I miss ewe moo and moo each day. ♥

The COW: nature's lawn moo-er

Virgin Wool... From sheep that run really fast

Thank Ewe From the Herd

23

King of the Porch

'Must Be' Puppy Love

Puppy Love Mini Scrapbook Page Directions (pictured on back cover)

Copy this page and the alphabet on pg 85 on white paper. Color the heart frame red and black. Color the letters to spell your dog's name red. Color small hearts on letters with a pink glitter pen. Use chalks to color puppy. Cut out and mat as shown.

Ti
To save tim
copy the alphabet o
red and color inside an
between the letters blac

Forever Faithful Friend

Doggone Good to T-bone

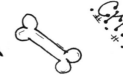

Our dog may be no perfect pedigree,
just the perfect mixture we agree...

A mutt!

MY DOG is MY BEST friend

HOME is WHERE YOUR DOG is

Tweet Dreams

Rent for a Song

Fly by night

Fly Right Inn

FOR WRENT! Cheap.cheap

Birdie Retweet

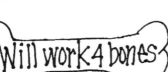

Will work 4 bones

Doggie Bag

DON'T LOOK! Bathing Birdies

Gone to the Dogs

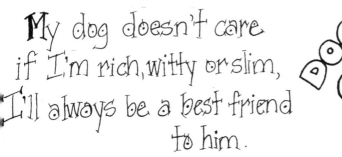

My dog doesn't care
if I'm rich, witty or slim,
I'll always be a best friend
to him.

DOG DROOL AFTERNOON

What's Mew?

Home is Where The Meow is

Critters

Welcome to the Cat House

I ♥ Birdies

Every life should have 9 cats!

TIGER in training

How wonderful to do nothing & rest afterwards

SLAVE to my CAT

My kitty makes everyday PURR-FECT

I'm not rude. I've got cat-i-tude!

In this house, The cat is in charge

smarty cat

FURRY TAILS MY FUR LADY

Pussed off!

Purr-ority Post Just for Mew Fur-class

Feline purr-fect tuna-night

27

Royal Family Scrapbook Page Directions (pictured on back cover)
Copy this page on gold marble cardstock. Use watercolor pencils and chalks to color everything, using methods on page 7.
Mat the title, expression and journaling on solid purple and gold mulberry. Mount on Francis Meyer #5006-973.

A FAMILY AFFAIR

FAMILY

We may not all be from the same family tree, But we make a good team Don't you agree?

MOTHERS have HEAVEN right UNDER THEIR FEET

If MOTHERS were FLOWERS I'd Pick YOU Again & Again

MOM

Thanks For Hatching Me

The King of the CASTLE And All His DIRTY RASCALS

My Mom is:
♥ My Guardian Angel
♥ My Heart Mender
♥ My Best Friend

FATHER OF THE YEAR

DAD
No Matter How Tall I Grow I'll Always Look Up To You

Mothers receive the highest pay PURE LOVE

Mother mender of Hearts

29

FAMILY

Our Family is a WORK of Heart

COUSINS are special friends grown from the same FAMILY tree

THIS ISN'T A SOAP OPERA... THIS IS ALL MY CHILDREN

Daddy;
You are my
favorite guy
to hold hands with

Sisterhood is Powerful

God couldn't be everywhere,
that's why he created Godparents

I've been blessed twice,
to call you my sister (brother mother father)
and a dear friend

Oh daughter (son) so dear,
We love you more than
   all the sand on the beach,
   stars in the sky and
   clothes on your floor!

My sister,
My friend

Dear Sister (or Brother)
Our childhood play days may
have come to an end...
But never forget,
You are forever my friend

Daughters
don't come any sweeter
than you

31

We Don't Remember Days
We Remember Moments
- Cesare Pavese

Large Old Fashioned Frame
Directions
(pictured on back cover)

Copy this page on gold marble cardstock.
The sample was colored with regular pencil
crayons. See page 7 for coloring tips.

Cut the inside of frame out.
Trim expression with decorative scissors.

Mat and mount on sage green and
black velvet as shown.

FAMILY IS ANOTHER NAME FOR LOVE

I may not be rich but I have some priceless jewels ... my grandchildren

Grandpas are like libraries.. Full of good stories.

Be humble? Impossible! Im the Grandparent

No picture gallery is richer in the happy images of children than a grandmother's ♡ heart ♡

- Helen Frank

Great Dads get promoted to Grand-dads

Family Reunions ♡ are ♡ ♡ Fabulous Fun ♡

GRANDPARENTS are Gods gift to Children

Best Gramps I ever saw.

CAUTION: Grandparents at Play

♡ Grandma's Sweethearts ♡

Work is for those who don't know how to fish

My Goal:
Fish more.
Work less.

Gone fishin'
Be back someday

Fishing
it's the reel thing

You catch...
You clean

Sounds a bit
fishy!

WELCOME TO THE LAKE

Reel Women Fish

An old fisherman
and the catch of his life
live here.

Captain's Quarters

Save
the Worms
Eat chicken

Hooked on Fishin'

Well stocked rivers, lakes and streams,
These are a fisherman's favourite dreams

If today were a fish, I'd throw it back.

35

Kindred Spirits

I cherish you
You're sweet and kind,
A truer friend I'll never find

Our frienship is like a cup of tea
a special blend of you ??? and me

You make my Heart Smile

True friends listen when no one else hears

Friendships are glued together with kindness

To get the full value of joy you must have someone to divide it with

Mark Twain

"Stay" is a charming word in a friend's vocabulary

- Mary Alcott

Back Door Friends Are Always Best

Share a Smile and Say Hello Exchange a Kindness and Watch a friendship GROW

Don't let grass grow on the path of friendship

- Native American Proverb

37

Friendship isn't a big thing.
It's a million little things

FRIENDS like you are far and few

Life is filled with simple joys
and blessings without end
but one of my greatest joys in life
is to count you as my dear friend.

I lost my smile and you gave me yours

Friends like you
do and say
the nicest things
in the sweetest way

FRIENDS HUG THE HEART

Friendship grows from pleasures shared.
- Charles Dickens

FRIENDS
♥ Share
♥ Support
♥ Laugh
♥ Love

Special Memories
are made with
Special Friends

The only way to have a friend is to be one.
- Ralph Waldo Emerson

39

I CAN RESIST ANYTHING...
EXCEPT TEMPTATION

Entering a Positive Thinking Area

Go ahead take my advice, I'm not using it anyway.

I'm saving my husband lot$ of money I BUY EVERYTHING I SEE... ON $ALE!

I'm not bald I'm just too tall for my hair

If you're smoking in this house you better be on fire!

If you smoke... don't exhale

You Don't have to BRUSH all your teeth Just the ones You want to KEEP

It's been one of those days ALL WEEK!

NoBRAIN...NoHeadache

Panic Button Press here.

A journey of 1000 steps begins with trying to find a parking spot.

Not again..... too much month at the end of the money

I'm so far behind I thought I was first

41

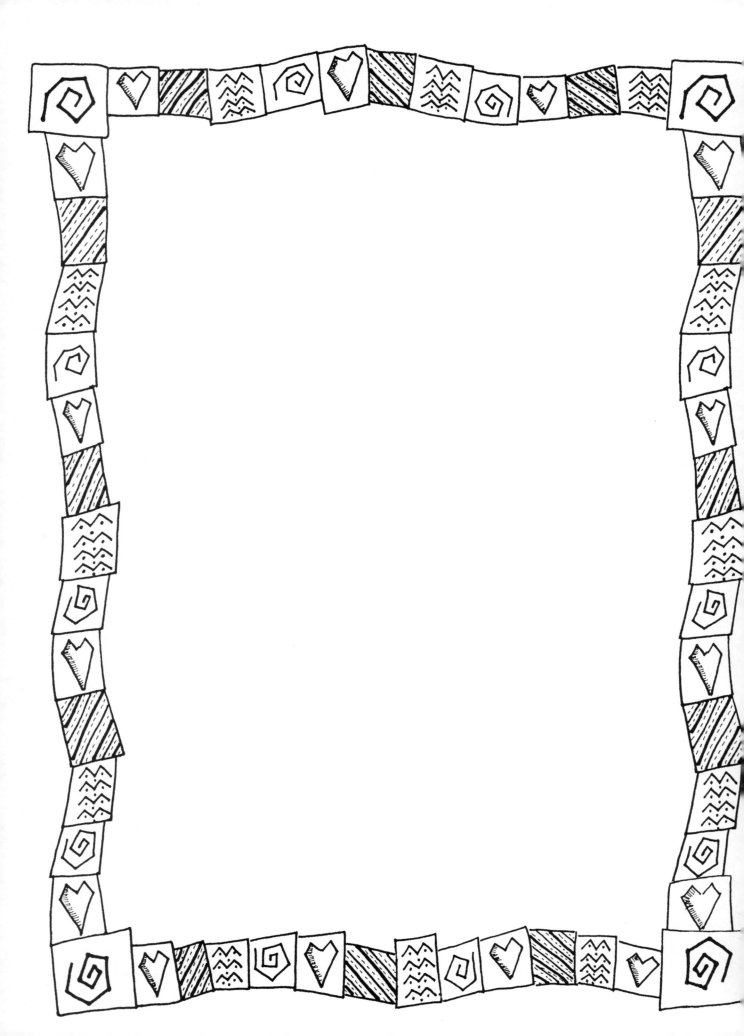

Macho doesn't prove Mucho

Real men DO ask directions.

HOME OF THE Lawn Ranger

Men are just a bunch of animals... but some do make good pets

Everytime I give my husband an inch he starts to think he's a ruler!

Only Mothers of teenagers can understand how animals can eat their young

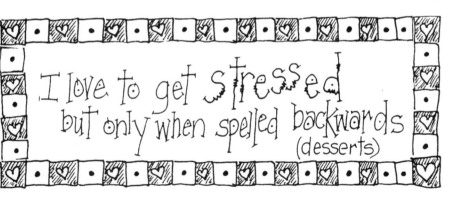
I love to get Stressed but only when spelled backwards (desserts)

SECRET TO DIETING spit out anything that tastes GOOD!

If the tv and the fridge weren't so far apart we'd never get any exercise

I'm not fat... I'm just short for my weight

Money is the root of all evil... and I need to feel rooted.

I am woman, I am invincible... I am tired.

Girls just wanna have fund$

43

My Garden Tills My Soul

Gardening

Everyone has a Mother-in-Nature

Have a Bloomin Good Day

Miracles grow where you plant them

Leave room in the Garden for Fairies to Dance

Gardening grows the Spirit

Nurture Nature

Flower Power

A garden is a friend you can visit anytime

I dig the earth

Like life, few gardens have only flowers

Nature wears a universal grin

Plant Some Kindness Wherever You Go

We may not have it all together...

but together we have it all

Garden Angels are Heaven Scent

Gardening

Garden of Love Recipe
- ♡ water with kindness
- ♡ nurture with compassion
- ♡ weed out resentment.

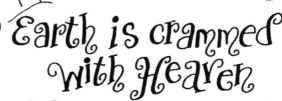

Earth is crammed with Heaven
Elizabeth Barrett Browning

A Sunset is Heaven's Gate Ajar

From the earth we were formed, to the earth we return.... and in between we garden

The touch of nature makes the whole world kin.
— William Shakespeare

One is nearer to God's heart in a garden, than anywhere else on earth
— Dorothy Gurney

We all need to be rooted in order to blossom

Nature is the art of God
— Dante

If you truly love nature you will find beauty everywhere
— Vincent Van Gogh

Heaven is under our feet as well as over our heads
— Henry David Thoreau

This garden is grown with love

My Best Chance For A Birdie

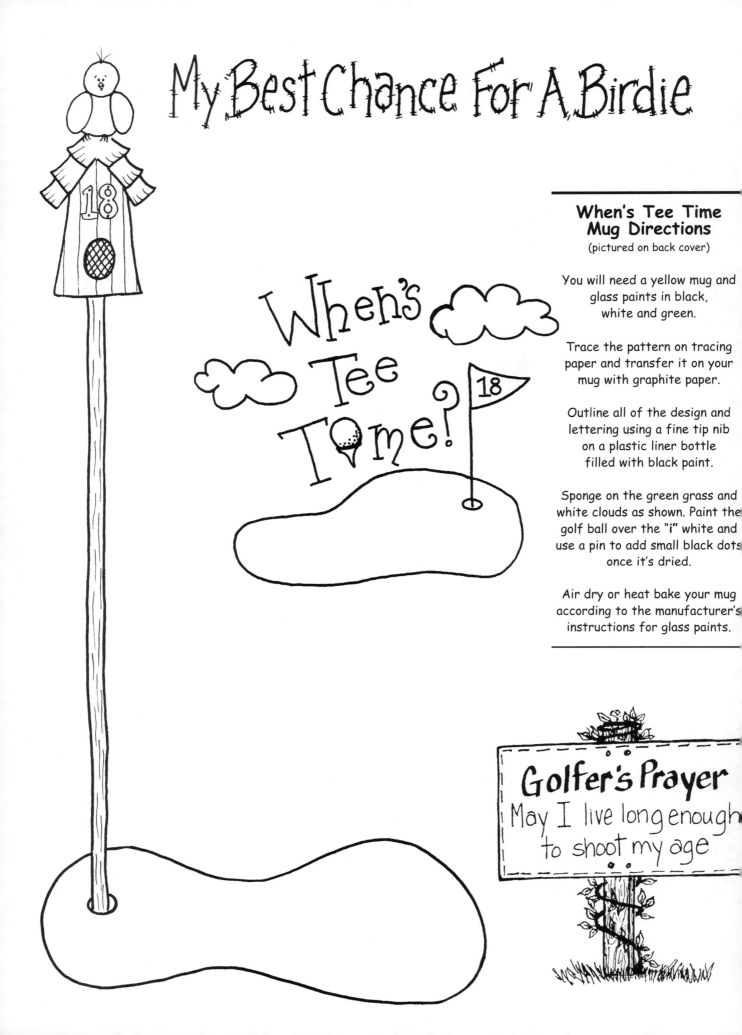

18

When's Tee Time?

18

When's Tee Time Mug Directions
(pictured on back cover)

You will need a yellow mug and glass paints in black, white and green.

Trace the pattern on tracing paper and transfer it on your mug with graphite paper.

Outline all of the design and lettering using a fine tip nib on a plastic liner bottle filled with black paint.

Sponge on the green grass and white clouds as shown. Paint the golf ball over the "i" white and use a pin to add small black dots once it's dried.

Air dry or heat bake your mug according to the manufacturer's instructions for glass paints.

Golfer's Prayer
May I live long enough to shoot my age

I used to WASTE my time, now I go GOLFING

Golfing

To golf or not to golf?
What a silly question

I ♥ GOLF

I GOLF
therefore I am not here

GOLFER'S
1
WISH

GOLF :
a day spent in a round
of strenuous idleness
- William Wordsworth

IRON MAN

Bye Bye Birdie

Queen
of the
Green

I'm not over the hill........ just on the back nine

Golf is a good walk spoiled.
- Mark Twain

I golf in the low 70's...
any colder I stay home

I live with fear everyday......
but sometimes she lets me go golfing

LEAN GREEN PUTTING MACHINE

Fangs for the memories and nightmares

GHOULS JUST WANNA HAVE FUN!

Come in for a bite

Pumpkins come. and pumpkins go ut jack-o-lanterns steal the show.

TOMB SWEET TOMB

WELCOME EVERY-Batty

HEY! I am THE Treat!

Love at 1st bite

COSTUME CUTIES

Fangtastic

The Ghostess With the Mostess!

Ghosts have real spirit!

Have A Hauntingly Happy Howl-ween

51

The journey of a thousand sites begins with a single click

The smell of fresh sawdust is sweeter to me, than any rose could ever be.

BEWARE COMPUTER BYTES!

Woodworkers are a cut above the board

Hunters lead a Wild life

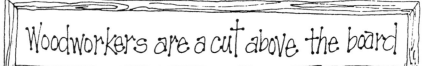

Rules 4 Tools
Put 'em back or catch the flack

Workshop Rule
Don't mess with my mess

Sew Some Sunshine

Dancers have happy feet!

Was there life B 4 Bingo

Quilts are pieces of love stitched together

I craft, therefore I am.

a stitch in time saves nine

Quiltin'

My Soul is Fed By Scrapbooking

Home is Where
We hang our
Memories

Home is where we hang our memories

HOME

Laughter is sunshine in a house

Bless this home with the music of laughter

Charity begins at home
- 14th century English proverb

Heaven seems a little closer in a house by the water

A small house can hold as much happiness as a large one.

Happiness is Home Brewed

Home is where our RV is

We get along in our R.V. cuz we don't have room to disagree.

HOME is the warmth of loving Hearts

Home to laughter home to rest, home to those we love the best!

Our guests make us happy, Some in coming, Some in going

Welcome to our Zoo!

WELCOME TO OUR "wRECK" ROOM A WILDLIFE REFUGEE HABITAT

55

ChoreList
Direct From The Queen Bee's

Name	Chore	Completed

Home Swept Home!

HOUSEWORK STINKS!

No — — — Martha Stewart does not live here.

Real men Do housework

House Rules

- If you open it.... close it
- If you empty it.... fill it up
- If you drop it.... pick it up
- If you spill it.... wipe it up
- If it rings.... answer it
- If it cries.... love it
- If you sleep in it.... make it up

Please excuse the mess. We just really want you to feel at home.

Every mother is a working mother

It's the maid's day off.... Don't trip on the dust balls

Cleaning your house
while your kids are still growing,
is like shovelling the walk
before it stops snowing.
— Phyllis Diller

Around here "normal" is just a setting on the dryer

A Place for Everything And Everything in its Place

— Isabelle Beeton, 1861

Whistle While You Work

— The Seven Dwarfs

The Queen does not do dishes

An open mind opens doors

Every life is a story...
make yours a Best
Seller.

Keep one secret spot
Where your dreams may go

Faith shines brightest in the dark

Problems are
Angels of
Opportunity

To discover new oceans
We must lose sight
of the shore.

We can't
spell
success
without
"U"

A journey of 1000 miles begins with but a single step
- Lao Tzu

Quitters never win
Winners never quit.

Dream deep,
    for dreams lie hidden in your soul
Reach high,
    for every dream precedes a goal.

Do the worst first!

Don't itch for anything
that you're not willing to scratch for.

Don't count the days, Make the days count.

Inch by inch
Any goal is a cinch

Carpe Diem
Seize the Day

View life by smiles,
not by tears
and age by
great moments,
not by years.

Happiness is
an inside job

No goals-
No glory

Mud thrown
is ground lost

Happiness
is just a smile away

We are all pencils
in the hand of a
writing God who is
sending love letters
to the world.
- Mother Teresa

Genius is
1% inspiration
99% perspiration
- Thomas Edison

Turn a frown upside down.

Don't
be-little.
Be Big.

heaven
is just the other
side of every
cloudy day

Laugh often,
Learn much
and love life
with all your
Heart

Opportunity never comes...It's here

Store recipes inside plastic
sheet protectors in a binder.

Recipe Name:

Source:

What to Put In:

Date:

How to Make It:

To create your own personal recipe
book make copies of this page.
Write or type your favorite recipes
on each page. Add any "Special
Stuff to Remember" like: " This is
my Mom's apple pie recipe, which
everyone LOVES! Her tip: Mix 2 or 3
types of apples together.

COVER THIS SPOT WITH A PHOTO
Example: Mom with her apple pie

Special Stuff to Remember:

Bless this Kitchen with Love & Laugter

The torch of Love
is lit in the Kitchen
Polish Proverb

God Blesses This Kitchen
He doesn't clean it

THIS CHICK IS COOKIN'

I ♥ love ♥ hugs,
I ♥ love ♥ kisses,
But don't forget,
I ♥ also ♥ love
HELP WITH THE DISHES.

Fish
to taste right
must swim
3 times...
~ in water
~ in butter
~ in wine
- French Proverb

I'd cook
if I could find the can opener

Happiness is lickin' the spoon

Spoonfuls of love added to every recipe.

Homemade with Love
from my kitchen.

Homemade and Good
4 - U - 2

63

Any Time Is Tea Time

Conserve Water.. Drink wine

Kitchen Quips

Wine is Sunlight Held Together By Water
- Galileo

I've never met a COOKIE I didn't like!

Sweety you're the 🥧 of my 🍎👁 (Sweety you're the pie of my eye)

FLOUR CHILD

Coffee Java

From One Bag To Another: You're Tea-RRIFIC!

Life is one big tea party

To bean or not to bean?

TEA THYME

Latte Da Latte Da...

Everything you see, I owe to spaghetti
- Sophia Loren

Money can't buy love... but it can buy caffè mocchas

I only have a kitchen cuz it came with the house

Peas be with you

Before my first cup of coffee I'm a bear!

I'm not a bad cook if you have no taste

65

Romantic Vellum Candle Wrap Directions
(pictured on back cover)

You will need a clear cylinder glass no larger than 3-1/4" in diameter,
so the vellum can cover the circumference. On plain white paper
trace heart frame in the center using a fine tip red Pigma marker.

Trace 'Love Lives Here' over the frame, using a chisel tip red Pigma marker.
Crop the photograph and glue it inside the heart frame.

Photocopy your page horizontally on a piece of 8-1/2" x 11" white vellum.
Trim it to wrap around glass and attach with double-sided tape.

Add water to glass and float a tea light candle.

Love Lives Here

I Made a Wish And You Came True

Consider Yourself Hugged!

Love means holding hands not grudges.

I love sharing life with YOU!

In the end the love you take is equal to the love you make.
- John Lennon

LIFE IS SO VERY FINE BECAUSE YOU ARE MY VALENTINE

Love is a hug

Forget love...
Let's fall in chocolate!

Love conquers all
- Virgil

Miles apart but always close in ♥

To love is to receive
A glimpse of heaven
- Karen Sunde

The happiest people in the world are the ones who help spread it!

The ♥ that loves is always young
- Greek Proverb

You make my heart flutter

Joy is a net of love
by which you can catch souls

Love can't grow
until you give some away

You take ordinary moments
and make them shine

One is very CRAZY
when in LOVE
- Sigmund Freud

Your love gives a glow to my soul

All works of love
are works of peace
- Mother Teresa

In all you dream
and all you do,
may the LOVE you share
bring sweet bliss to you

XOX
You paint
my world
with
Love

Loved you yesterday,
love you still,
always have and
always will

All you need is love
- John Lennon

You complete me
- Jerry MaGuire

You are so easy
to love

Love wasn't put in your heart to stay
Love isn't love until you give it away

A Match Made in Heaven

This album was created so you would always see,
Why you mean the world to me.

You Have A Piece of My Heart

TAKEN

A STORY BOOK ROMANCE

Under the Spell of Love

May yours be the best love story ever told,
A rich tapestry of happy memories to have and to hold.

Hearts forever entwined

I DO I DO I DO I Love You

Seasons come and Seasons go Captured here are the Sweetest Memories We Know

6 Cupid Strikes Again

Heading Down Memory Lane

FORGET ME NOT

Memories are forget-me-nots
Gathered along life's way,
Pressed close to the heart
In a perennial bouquet
— Clara Smith Reber

Memories
are windows
that bring the past
into view
where we can glimpse again
all the joys we ever knew

We Don't Remember Days
We Remember Moments
— Cesare Pavese

Memory is a Painter
It Paints Pictures of The Past
— Grandma Moses

The Heart is Like a Garden
Where Sweet Memories Grow
With Life's Best Moments
Tended Row by Row

Dream Weaver

Memory
is the
Treasure
of all things
and their
Guardian
— Cicero

The soul would have no
rainbow if the eye
had no tear

Keepsakes

MEMORIES

Family memories and stories retold
are like treasures as dear as gold

Who has not saved some trifling thing
more prized than jewels rare,
a faded flower, a broken ring,
a tress of golden hair
— Ellen Howarth

The Memories
We Collect & Give
Brighten our Lives
as Long As We Live
— Julie Sneyd

73

Oh the Experince of this Sweet Life
- Dante

over the hill

VALUABLE HISTORIC MONUMENT

I'm a valuable antique with hair full of silver teeth full of gold and joints full of lead

THE OVER the HILL GANG

For the unlearned old age is winter. For the learned it is the season of harvest — The Talmud

Look 30, Act 20, Feel 60 Must be 40

It takes a long time to grow old
- Pablo Picasso

Age is only a number and mine is unlisted

Been there, Done that... Can't remember

I'M NOT OVER the HILL I CAN'T GET UP IT!

HAPPY 29... again?

I'm too young to be this old !

I shall grow old but never lose lifes zest, because the roads last turn shall be the best.
- Henry Van Dyke

Grow old along with me, the best is yet to be.
- Robert Browning

LIFE is the greatest bargain,
We get it for nothing
— Yiddish

Do good and heaven will come down to you.
— Hawaiian

A stumble
may prevent a fall
— Chinese

The best candle is
understanding.
— Welsh

You make the road by walking on it.
— Nicaraguan

The more you know,
The less you need
— Austrailian Aboriginal

KIND WORDS CONQUER
— Asian

The day is lost
if no one has
laughed.
— French

The flowers of all tomorrows
are in the seeds of today.
— Asian

Before you marry,
keep both eyes open
After marriage,
shut one.
— Jamaican

It takes a 1000 voices
to tell a single story.
— Native American

New day.... New fate
— Bulgarain

If you are lucky enough to be Irish,
you are lucky enough.
— Irish fact

God works in Moments

Profound Proverbs

Beauty without virtue is...
a flower without perfume.
- French

EARTH IS DEARER THAN GOLD
- Estonian

FAITH KEEPS THE WORLD GOING
- Hindi

Good deeds
re the best prayer.
- Serbian

Worry often gives
a small thing a
BIG SHADOW

I LIVE a MAN WITH DISHPAN HANDS
- Kitchen Proverb

A gentle word
opens an iron gate.
- Bulgarian

Hold a true friend with both
your hands
- Nigerian

In dreams and in love
nothing is impossible
— Hungarian

Trust in God.....
but tie up your camel
- Iranian

Make haste slowly
Latin Proverb

No sleep....
No dreams.
- Korean

It is better to be in chains
with friends,
than in a garden with strangers
- Persian

79

All Star

Best Team in Town

Sports

You're an ALL STAR in our Hall of Fame

FLYING THROUGH THE AIR WITH THE GREATEST OF EASE

TEAM SPIRIT

A Shootin' Star

Go Team!

Hockey Players Stick Together

NHL Here I Come!

#1

FANATICAL FAN!

Magic Skates

The Smell of Victory

MVP

☆ Grandpa's All Stars ☆

81

Beary Best Buds

Happy Bearday

Don't feed us
We're stuffed.

Stuffed with Love

Best Fur-ends
Fur-ever

A friend by your side
Can keep you warmer
than any fur coat

Friends ... make everything bearable

Show Me
the Honey

FREE BEAR HUGS
anytime...
any bear

Honey Bee Happy

Bear
with
me

Bear Collector
Orphans Welcome.

I wish I was a teddy bear...
The more worn out you are
The more valuable you become.

Only the most
Special Bears
get their fur all
loved off

Baskets Full of Easter Joy for Every Little

Girl & Boy

Life's a Beach Scrapbook Page Directions

(pictured on back cover)

Copy page 85 on plain white paper. Cut out the expressions and graphics you want to use and glue them on plain paper, leaving enough space over and under 'Life's a Beach' for journaling and the layered sand effect.

Copy page on light colored sand card stock. Color the lettering and graphics with water color pencils. See page 7 for coloring tips. Mat photo on orange or a suitable color and mount on Carolee's Creations Robin Egg Blue.

To create the layered sand, you also need a blank piece of dark sand cardstock. Hold both together, and carefully tear, pulling towards you. Mount the darker sand behind and above the light piece with the expression. Glue the beach graphics in between the sand layers.

Fun in the Sun

Dolphin Boy

Little Mermaid

WAVE RIDER

LIFE'S A BEACH!

Shore Fun Times

Just Pooling Around

ABCDEFGHI
JKLMNOPQ
RSTUVWXYZ
1234567890
abcdefghij
klmnopqrs
tuvwxyz

My Favourite Spot

There is a place
in my childhood
I remember well,
full of joy and happiness
and wonderful tales to tell
A place where loving memories
were passed along to me,
When I was in my
favourite spot
upon my Grandma's knee.

Sandy Redburn

Pricless Treasures

Sharing Love
Finding a true friend
Giggling children
The beauty of nature
A proud moment
A prayer answered
Our sweet memories

Sandy Redburn

May your joys
be as bright
as the morning
Your years of happiness
as numerous
as the stars in the heavens
and your sorrows
but shadows,
that fade in the sunlight
of your love

- Old Wedding Blessing

Garden Memories

A garden unearths
part of our childhood
of backyard memories
and everything good
Of marvelous mud pies,
rocks and bugs,
mending scraped knees
with Mothers hugs.
But most of us can best recall,
picking a fistful of flowers
with magical powers
to light up our
Mothers face

Sandy Redburn